The Cleaner Fish

Gordon Meade

ARROWHEAD
PRESS

First published 2006 by:
Arrowhead Press
70 Clifton Road, Darlington,
Co. Durham, DL1 5DX
Tel: (01325) 260741

Typeset in 11pt Laurentian by
Arrowhead Press

Email: editor@arrowheadpress.co.uk
Website: http://www.arrowheadpress.co.uk

ISBN 1-904852-10-6

Arrowhead Press acknowledges the financial assistance of
Arts Council England, North East

Arrowhead Press is a member of
Independent Northern Publishers

Printed by Athenaeum Press, Gateshead, Tyne and Wear.

For Wilma and Sophie

"Hope is the thing with feathers
That perches in the human soul."

- Emily Dickinson.

Acknowledgements

Thanks are due to the editors of the following publications in which some of these poems have appeared:

Another Book to Burn,
Balancing on a Barbed Wire Fence,
Black Mountain Review,
Cencrastus,
Chapman,
The Eildon Tree,
Flaming Arrows,
The Interpreter's House,
Island,
Lines Review,
New Writing Scotland 12 and 16,
Nomad,
Northwords,
Open World III,
The Order of Things,
Other Poetry,
Poetry Salzburg,
Poetry Scotland,
Resurgence,
Rubens,
Spring into Fall,
Spume,
Storm,
Verse,
West Coast Magazine.

Cover image:
Glass bottle in the shape of a fish, El Amarna, Egypt, c. 1350 BC.
© The Trustees of the British Museum

Contents

Contents ~ continued

III.

IV.

I

A Bumblebee

I spent the whole morning.
Well, no, not the whole morning,
just a breakfast,

in silence,
in sitting,
in listening

to the others;
to those gathered
round the table;

to those rooted
in the earth outside;
and to those flying

about in the open air.
I listened, and I listened,
and I listened.

But still I was unaware
as to what it was I was
hearing. As I opened

the kitchen door to leave,
I met myself in the guise
of a bumblebee,

banging my head,
repeatedly, against
a pane of glass.

The Song of the Chough

The song of the chough
is little more than a cough;

the nervous sort a poet might give
before he starts to read from his latest work;

or the polite kind a doctor might give
before he imparts the dreadful news.

But the chough is never a muse.
At best, her song is a slight irritation

at the back of the throat;
something that clears the air,

to make way,
for the main event.

The Song of the Skylark

The song of the skylark is his life. It is
also his great work and, as with Sisyphus,
it is also a boulder which, with lungs and wings,
he tries to roll uphill, on invisible thermals,

and always fails. And yet, his very failure
is also a success; it is a chance to start again;
to sing once more. And at what point, do you think
is he most the skylark? Not when the song is

complete; not at the top of the arc
of sound; not at the beginning when he is
merely composing himself for the ascent. No,
it is all in the process; all in the attempt.

The Song of the Woodpecker

The song of the woodpecker is nothing
if not persistent. If he does his own head in
by continually battering it against the bark,
then he does mine in too, just by making me
listen to it. If only he would stop. It is a form

of solid Chinese water torture. Not drip,
drip, drip; but knock, knock, knock. The results
of his brain scan should be known this month.
Apparently, the right and left hemispheres have
merged to make a whole; the objectless object;

the goal of all meditation. Unfortunately,
for me, this has not led on to the sound of one
hand clapping. Who would have believed that
enlightenment could be achieved by abuse
of such an extreme order? Who would have

guessed it would have caused so much din?

The Song of the Raven

The song of the raven is a harsh sort of music,
a rapid burst from a Kalashnikov, that drowns out
the other gentler rhythms of the coast. It comes

from above the cliffs and drifts down towards me
where I stand at the edge of the sea contemplating
nothing. And that is all she brings me; no lessons
from the past; no hopes for the future; not even

the stark realisation of where I am in the here
and now. And yet, she does manage to make me
more aware of the facts. She can fly through the air

on jet-black wings, whereas I can hardly even stand
my ground. She can move with a kind of awkward grace,
whereas I merely stumble over rocks. And she can sing,
after a fashion, whereas I find it almost impossible

to talk. In the end, she was the right bird,
and at the right time. A heron would be far
too spiritual; a crow would not be enough.

The Redshank

The neurotic of the rock-pool, the maniac
of the coast, how much energy do you think he has
lost just in trying to hold himself together?

When startled, his cry almost rips him apart.
Like muscle torn from the lining of his heart it flies
to his throat and his legs collapse. Yet still,

his wings encourage flight. He lands just out
of sight of whatever it was that scared him. Examining
his reflection in the salt, he is somewhat reassured

by the drabness of his coat. But then, he catches
a glimpse of his shocking legs and, once again, he is off;
convinced in a split-second, he is drenched in blood.

The Hanged Guillemot

Found on a farm in Inverin,
a guillemot hanging by her ankles
from a branch of ash

with a flag as red
as the food of the dead
draped above her head.

And was she a warning
from the farmer to his hens
to keep on laying?

Or was she a gift for the fox
that might come in the middle
of the night and slay them?

Or was she a fisherman's totem
hung up in the diving position to prevent
unwanted storms at sea?

Or was she merely decoration;
a brilliance of black and white
to brighten a dying tree.

The Night Heron

Tonight, I am sleeping across the road
from the animals in the zoo. Tonight, I am
aware that beyond the drone of lorries

and cars, the representatives of the wild
are snoring; are dreaming of their freedom.
But there is one inmate, who thinks

that he has got it made, the night heron,
who sleeps safe inside the zoo all day, and then
takes off at night to enjoy the fishy delights

of the local ponds and lakes. Tomorrow
morning, pre-dawn, when I am struggling
to awake, to ready myself for flight,

he, too, will be winging his way
back to his chosen open prison; a taste
of freedom decomposing in his gut.

Puffins

Our little brothers and sisters
of the north find out soon enough
what it means to thrive in darkness.
It's the first couple of months

in the burrow that does it.
So that, when they grow up, they do
so with "traditional family values".

Keep your head down
son, and do the business.

They mate for life, man and wife,
and try to keep their children safe
from the neighbours. But, just like us,
they have their other side. They do

belly flops in the Forth just for fun,
and raise their rainbow beaks as one
to greet the morning sun. Black

on top and white below,
what you cannot see, they are

not going to show. They fly better
underwater than they do through air,
and bring back fish, ten at a time,
to show their kids how much they care.

Eight Bird Dreams

The house sparrow dreams of adventure
 and trans-continental flights; while

the swallow dreams of a night by the fire,
 with the telly, the kids and the wife.

The raven dreams in colour of Picasso,
 of Chagall and of Klimt; while

the parakeet dreams in black and white
 of *News At Ten* and *Books in Print*.

The cormorant dreams of *Vogue* magazine
 and five-point-nine for dives; while

the heron dreams of *Ecstasy*, of raves
 and the flash of knives.

The owl dreams of *The Beach Boys*, of lager
 and the sun on his back; while

the skylark dreams of a nightcap,
 of silence and the dark.

The Cuckoo

To begin with, I was just the same
as any other bird, but after my abandonment
in a stranger's nest, something

even stranger began to take shape.
First of all, I realised that I was larger than
my brothers and sisters; larger even

than the odd couple that appeared
to be my parents. I also discovered that
I had been given a strong back

and a powerful pair of shoulders,
with which I was able to pitch my smaller
siblings up and out of the family

nest. Soon, there was no room
left, not even for my surrogate mother
and father. In the end, they just

stood in amazement as I, their
adopted offspring, opened up my pair
of outsize wings and sauntered off.

The Eagle
(after Prometheus)

For me to say that I caught his attention
would have to be the biggest understatement
of the year. For who wouldn't have, with my beak
buried in his liver, with my talons hooked

inside his chest. But to say that I earned
his respect, I would have to be a little more
circumspect. For how could he respect me, I, who
had shown him, so blatantly, the extent

of his own ambitions. And yet, I gave him
what only an eagle can give. Not what he was
looking for; he thought he had already found that;
but what would happen to him if he ever did.

The Mask of the Heron

I could adopt the mask of the heron.
I could uproot its plume of feathers
and wear it on my head as either a halo,
or a lightning-rod, as something to attract
a form of enlightenment, or failing that,

the wrath of God. I could snap off
its pointed beak and raise it to my mouth
to use as either a reed, or a loud-hailer,
as anything through which the gods
within might either breathe, or speak.

The Cage
for Jack Withers

1.

Last night, I heard tell of a cage,
perched on a hill, made to catch crows.
Baited with a sheep's carcass, its sides slanted down
towards an inviting gap to trap unwary scavengers.
Lured by the stench of rotten flesh, all they could do
was wait until the farmer came with his .22.

2.

Shot through the head, the crows
were then hung, upside-down on a barbed-
wire fence or, nailed by their wings to the farm's
barn-door as a warning to others - NO LAMB
STEALERS TOLERATED ON THESE COLD MOORS.

3.

A horrendous tale, a horror story.
But more horrendous; the workings of the mind
that spawned the thought; the body that sprouted
the feet that walked towards the spot; the hands
that made the cage; and the fingers that pulled
the trigger that fired the shot.

4.

Tremendous, the blackness of crows,
so natural; terrific, the whiteness of sheep,
so abused; horrendous and horrific,
the unnatural greyness of man.

II

The Harbour, Eyemouth

Whenever I hear gulls
it reminds me of here;

as if this is the only place
I have ever really heard them;

as if the gulls here know something
that gulls elsewhere can only imagine;

something I need to know;
something only they can tell me.

Winter Storms

The December sea threatens
to enter our homes; has leapt
the harbour walls, and soaked

the sandbags laid at every door.
Even the straight line of the horizon
is ragged with storm; each wave

breaking like the shattered glass
on the face of a smashed alarm.
The sky darkens, and the sea

becomes our dark unknown.
Fears of drowning surface out
of the depths of sunken dreams.

We wake to waves crashing,
and rivers bursting banks that once
contained nothing but streams.

Mist

for Stuart Syme

A forest of pine trees felled
by mist, uprooted by vapour, and rendered
invisible by particles of water,

suspended in air. Cattle isolated,
removed from their herds in pockets of fog.
Ewes losing their lambs. Loosed

from their mothers' moorings,
wrapped in damp blankets, their shallow
bleats carry like foghorns through

the fading light. Beneath the city's
twin bridges, a river of seals flows slowly
onwards, water confined by banks.

As it reaches the estuary, moved
by the moon, it relinquishes the illusive land,
for the salt-water clarity of sea.

The Night Pools

Now, after over twelve years' living
on the coast, I have started to explore
its pools by night. Torch in hand,

I clamber stealthily across its seaweed-
covered rocks, looking for the reflected glimmer
of substantial bodies of liquid salt.

Beneath the torchlight's shaft of white,
the night fish freeze. With ease, I can trap a Cornish
Sucker with a single flick of my wrist.

The only trouble is that both of us are
caught; the fish, too petrified to move, in case
the blinding light conceals a heron's

thrust; and I, unwilling to extinguish
my Medusa's stare, in case the moment
of shared fear, prematurely, is lost.

Bochum : The Botanical Gardens
for Dieter Wessels

We have been led in and out
of every imaginable landscape;

trekked through tundra, clambered over
alps, navigated coastlines, and plunged,
wet-shirted, into jungles, to reach
this place of contradiction - an oriental
temple in the heart of the West -

where water talks to water
about the softness of rock.

The Cleaner Fish

In a fish tank, in a pub, in the middle
of the worst winter in thirty years, two cleaner
fish are going about their business of polishing glass
with their lips. They are blind to whatever

it is that lies beyond their man-made
horizons. They are oblivious to the other fish
with whom they share their prison. They just get on
with doing what it is that they do best; clearing
a surface for others to look into the depths.

The Common Carp
for Desmond Graham

An uncommon fish;
in Japanese, a homophone
of love;

in Chinese,
literary skill; a carp that's leapt
the Dragon Gate, a man adept
with ink and quill.

In both; true
courage in the face
of fate.

Long-lived,
and sensitive to sound,
producing its own song deep
within its pond.

Our love
of water, common
ground.

The Grey Whale

The grey whale has a heart.
Just like us, the grey whale has a heart,
and it is the size of a family car.

The grey whale has blood vessels.
Just like us, the grey whale has blood
vessels and, with care, we could

swim through them. We could
dip our toes in its veins. We could
wash our fingers in its arteries.

The grey whale has a tongue.
Just like us, the grey whale has a tongue,
and it is the weight of an elephant.

The grey whale has a voice.
Just like us, the grey whale has a voice
and it can travel, through the depths,

for miles. When the grey whale
opens its mouth to speak, we would
do well to listen to its song.

The Shark

To have a life so well honed down
as a shark's; where the merest whiff of blood
acts as a trigger to release one's

non-thinking, totally instinctual,
predatory gifts. To be able to dismiss
thought; to get rid of all one's

psycho-babble, the white noise
of the human species, and just exist. No Freud,
no Jung, no Melanie Klein; just

the pure line of a fin through salt.
To offload Shakespeare and unplug Bach; to have
never seen a Rembrandt, nor a Monet,

nor a Braque. To be one's own work
of art, a one-man show, a performance piece, a word-
less monologue of cartilage and teeth.

With no beginnings to be grateful
for, and no endings to fear. To be able just
to live; right now, right here.

Vultures

They are neither the starter, nor
the main course. They are not even
the dessert. They are what comes after;
indigestion, angina, the attack.

After the pride's self-satisfied
purring; after the pack's nervous
laughter; what you will hear will be
their beaks, snapping shut.

And they have bided their time,
up in the branches of the acacia tree.
Baking, slowly, in the noon-day sun, they
have waited patiently. They have

had to endure the lionesses' prime cuts;
the hyenas' cracking bones. But, in the end,
they will descend, with their feigned gratitude,
for the gristle, which is theirs alone.

The Florida Alligator

Alligators' eyes deaden with age;
and how these dinosaurs age.

From young whippersnappers
of no more than a foot or two, through
to adolescent yards, and on to adult metres.
And their eyes grow with them.

What in the young were beetle-black,
become less glossy, almost black, and turn,
in adults, into clouded glass.

They do not need to see so much,
and have nothing to fear but themselves.
Alligators are not as short-sighted as they would
have us believe. It suits their purposes.

Their eyelids close when their jaws shut
and their bodies corkscrew through the water
of the Everglades. Surfacing with

a slow-motion blink, they know that
their Earth still turns very nicely on its rusty
axis; that all is well with the world in which they
find themselves; the world they made.

The Florida Panther

The Florida panther is not,
of course, a real panther,

in the same way as the land
of the free has been manufactured
out of the bones of its owners.

The Florida panther is a mountain lion,
but it is a mountain lion without a mountain.
What it has in common with a real panther
is the eyes. One, lounging, head-height,

on the bough of a cypress, turned
her head and looked right through me.

And I mean right through; as if
those eyes had x-ray vision. I could
feel her gaze penetrate the back

of my skull and then move on. Later,
I chose to flatter myself by thinking that
she had somehow recognized my existence;
had somehow realised I had been there too.

The Florida Heron

My heron; my poor grey heron;
my bird of sackcloth and ashes; my bird
of eternal mourning; has been transformed.
To be honest, in the beginning, he was
just the same as he was back home;

almost invisible against a backdrop
of rushes. But when I saw him next,
he had been bleached white by the Florida
sun, and emerged from behind a curtain
of saw grass like a lighthouse on stilts,

proclaiming not, "Catch me if you can!",
but, "Look! Look over here! Here I am!"
I saw him again, later that day, slightly more
subdued, turning a deep purple, as the sun
sank crimson into the waters of the Gulf.

But, it was his final manifestation
I admired the most; still grey-winged,
but green-backed; smaller than before, but
braver; no longer tiptoeing through water
lilies and bullfrogs, but striding out

between the dozing snouts of alligators.

Egrets

I am unaware whether they are
the representatives of the inner heron
or just their disembodied ghosts; and for a bird
I had never seen, until today, there are too many
of them to decide. We see them at the side

of the dirt road, between the camp-
site and the cook-house, trying to hide
in the man-sized reeds, or alighting on the backs
of alligators, just for the thrill. They are beautiful after-
thoughts, added to a drab landscape to illuminate

the artist's skill. They are silent; birds
of snow that should have melted long ago
underneath the Florida sun. One by one, they rise
and fall, as if on low-level thermals. Somehow, they don't
look tough enough to survive out here, in the land

of the diamond-backed rattlesnake
and the snapping turtle. And, indeed,
many of them have lost their legs, and more,
in the shallows of the mangroves. Slight, white angels,
they appear in the midday mirages and evaporate

as the air cools. Towards dusk, their places
are taken by the bats and the owls. They spend
their nights reapplying coats of brilliant white to their
fading plumage. In the morning, they will return to outshine
the morning sun; each one a lighthouse beam

of feathers; a snowflake of muscle and bone.

III

Mount Beckwith
for Watty and Linda

To start with, this is not my sort
of landscape. There is not enough water
in it; a minor river that reflects

only the lines of reeds that borders
its slowly flowing edges; sedge, or some such plant.
The pines in the distance are

more attractive. They have become
my *dark woods*, a place I would love to be lost in;
knowing that the mountain would be

waiting once I had crossed over
the fallen needles. At night, I can see it all
from my pillow. The beauty of it

lies in the azure sky; the perfect blue
sky of childhood. Not the one we lived through,
but the one we wished we had;

the lapis lazuli of unconditional love.

North of Normal

Our shaman keeps
his second skin inside
an open sardine tin.

He wraps a fish
within a shroud just to confuse
the puzzled crowd.

He pins a crow's head
on a knife just to remind us
there's a point to life.

He spikes an oak leaf
on a thorn to tell us we all have
to die in order to be born.

He nails a Catherine wheel
through a white asbestos glove to show us
the beauty and the price of love.

Symbols of Survival :
after Will Maclean

Symbols of Survival

It's there

in the grain,
in the carved,
polished wood.

It's there

in the rolled
canvas apron, in the open
pockets of pine.

It's there

in the harpoons,
in the pork-rind, in the printed
instructions.

The life

of the imagination
survives everything,
even the skull

of a porpoise.

Fisherman Listening for Herring

It's found
in the sound,
in the quality

of the noise they make
leaping clear from water.

It's etched on the face
of a ring-net fisherman,

all eyes and ears,
hopes and fears,
listening for silver.

Raft of the Medusa II

It's set   in a frame   of blood-

stained   wood

scored   by cutlasses.

On the raft   of the Medusa II,

the last   of the survivors

fought   for a taste

of lemon,   while beneath

the waves,   the fish

preyed   for more   substantial food.

The Four Elements

(i)

I have stood in the fire
    but you were the one
        who was burnt.

I have plunged into water
    but you were the one
        who was drowned.

I have walked on the earth
    but you were the one
        who was buried.

I have flown through the air
    but yours were the wings
        on which I was carried.

(ii)

I have raked the embers of the fire
    and seen your bleached bones
        turning in the ashes.

I have trawled the ocean's darkness
    and seen your bloated body
        raised in tangled nets.

I have tilled the ploughed-up soil
    and seen in each flower that blossomed
        your eyes' dark pupils.

I have flown into the strongest wind
    and felt your wing-beats
        brushing my skin.

Sea Levels

A ladder
> of levels
a stairwell
> of depths.

A flight
> of fathoms
a landing
> of deaths.

A spiral
> of metres
a storey
> of nets.

A Plimsoll
> of tidemarks
a world
> without breath.

Beluga Blue

Out of kingfisher   by peacock,

out of turquoise   by cyan,

out of eggshell   by duck-egg,

out of cobalt   by Prussian.

Out of cornflower   by bluebell,

out of hyacinth   by smalt,

out of Oxford   by Cambridge,

out of gentian   by perse.

Out of midnight   by navy,

out of azure   by bice,

out of pale   by livid,

out of sapphire   by ice.

Thirty-Six Creatures :

Eleven Sea Anemones and One Coral

Snakelocks   Beadlet   Dahlia

Burrowing   Strawberry   Cloak

Plumose   Gem   Daisy

Parasitic   Jewel   Cup

A Dozen Worms

Square-tailed   Bootlace   Arrow

Honeycomb   Green Leaf   Keel

Horsehair   Peanut   Parchment

Red Ribbon   Peacock   Scale

Eleven Crabs and One Goby

Hairy	Edible	Hermit
Spider	Porcelain	Masked
Swimming	Spiny	Thornback
Velvet	Shore	Black

A Walk through Seaweed

Through coral weed
               and sea oak,
through sea lettuce
               and thongweed.

Through sugar kelp
               and eel grass,
through dabberlocks
               and oarweed.

Through rainbow bladder
               and knotted wrack,
through furbelow
               and cuvie.

Through purple laver
               and pepper dulse,
through mermaid's tresses
               and Irish moss.

IV

Inside the Stomach of a Cow

1. The Rumen

To begin with; in the beginning;
at the start; very close to the heart,
lies the rumen. And it is a place.
It is a place just like any other.

It is a place in which we can ruminate.
It is a place in which we can chew the cud.
It is a place in which we can mull things over.
It is a place in which we can contemplate.

It is also a sack of fingers. It is
a sack of fingers in which we can turn
things over, and over, and over. It is a sack
of fingers in which we can get to know

the feel of how things are, the feel
of how things were, and the feel of how
things might be. It is a sack of fingers in which
we can get to grips with our dreams.

2. The Reticulum

What happens next is what comes
after. And what comes after usually
happens because of what went before.
And because what happens has to happen,
this is where we find ourselves, now;

stuck in a cell, caught in a net, jammed
in a honeycomb. And this is where we become
one of a swarm of bees, a single part of a hive
of industry. We become drones; we become
workers; we become movers and shakers;

makers of homes. And, while here, it
becomes our task to sub-divide; to realise
our limitations; to remain the same and be left
behind, or to continue on our way in whichever
shape or form we might just have in mind.

3. The Omasum

And this, then, is the third
dimension. This is volume number three.
This is where the words get written down;
words like love and hate, words

like you and me. This is a filter,
and we are the filter-feeders, eager not
to miss a single drop of whatever it is that is being
swirled around. Here, we are closer

to the ground. This is the birth-
place of both fiction and fact; sometimes
known as the butcher's bible because it looks so
like a book. This is the penultimate

act. This is where words become
phrases. This is where phrases lie down
together on pages. And this is where pages are
bound; but bound into what?

4. The Abomasum

And this is where the past has taken
us, as ever, only so far. Whether or not it
was where we wanted to be taken,

this is where we have had to come.
Eventually, in the end, after all has been said
and done, after all the tripe; after all

the honey, and after all the waffle;
this is where we come to be broken down,
and to recover. This is the rennet-

bag. This is where everything gets
absorbed. This is where everything gets
reduced to order. And this is where

everything that matters, including
matter itself, gets transformed into energy;
but not before it has been dissolved.

Death Caps

They grew up overnight, on that I would swear.
When I walked out along this narrow path, the ground
beneath my feet was cold and bare. But now, there is a rash
of them, a mass of domed profusion. And though

I know there are so many I might choose, I do
not know their names and fear, whichever one I plump
for, I may lose. Yet still, I press one to my lips and chew.
The taste is somewhat pallid but the texture is rich

and smooth. It goes down easy. It goes down
easy like a swallowed hook. I retch and I splutter. I try
to spit the whole lot out, then rearrange it on the earth
when it does come up. Eventually, I am pleased that

all the tiny fragments have come out - a fungal
jigsaw of a mushroomed trip. But what about the hook,
I hear you quip. The hook? Alas, the truth will out. The hook
is still stuck inside the lining of my mouth.

The Dying

What to do with the dying?
The dead are easy. They can either be
buried or consumed by flames.

The living are fine, too. They can
either be cared for or be abandoned
with a clear conscience.

But the dying still have claims
on us. They can still shout. They can
still whimper. They can entreat.

And they can shame. Of the three,
I think that I am happiest with the living,
but after them it is definitely

the dead. The dying have the look
of prison warders about them; only
the dead can set you free.

The Sundown Lounge

Apparently there is a bar somewhere
in small town America, perhaps in the mid-West,
perhaps in Idaho, where lost souls go as they wait
to be told, to where they will be sent.

They call the bar The Sundown Lounge, not
Limbo, as you might have thought, as they cater
for all religions. It is always Happy Hour at Sundown,
though you wouldn't guess it from the faces

on the clientele. No one talks at all.
They just keep on drinking, for they know
that when 'last orders' are called at Sundown,
they'll all be kicked out to their individual

heaven or their individual hell, or back
to the world they knew as human in another skin;
maybe with an extra pair of legs, or a set of streamlined
wings, or maybe with a rattle in their tail.

Nana

I am small enough
for the bed I am sitting on
to be big enough for me to be able
to be far enough away from her
for her to be unable to get near me.

But, as ever, I have
sat too close. No words are
spoken. Fear has silenced me and,
somehow, her voice-box is broken.
Slowly, she strokes the back of my hand

with her bony fingers
as mine bunch, automatically,
into a fist. She grabs my wrist and
squeezes. I sit there, looking out
the window at a crow swallowing a lump

of bread. To all intents
and purposes, from the neck
down, I am dead. I feel no pain. I am
all eyes, and both of them are
focussed on the blackness of the crow.

The Summer Son

During the summer, I would sit
myself down in the middle of the lounge
and raise my hand up to the beam of light that shone
through the crack in the velvet curtains.

There, I would examine the delicate
tracery of my bones, the redness of my skin,
the blueness of my veins; each one illuminated by
that single ray of the sun. With my eyes,

I would follow the particles of dust
as they danced around, and in between,
my slowly moving fingers. Gradually, I grew to love
that solitary shaft of light framed,

as it was, by all those folds of darkness.

Cars

1.

On some days, my mother would stare
at me as if she were looking through the crumpled wreckage
of a car, peering through the smashed windows, hoping
that inside there was someone she still recognized, someone
that she could love. Then, like a startled rabbit, she would
recoil, appalled at the darkness of her desires.

2.

I had a passion too, for breaking my toys,
especially my favourite Dinky cars, the ones my father
would give me each Friday afternoon when he came home
from the market. After an especially heated row

with my mother, I would carry one or two
of them to the box-room upstairs, hurl them against
the walls, stamp on them until they were almost flat, and then
pull off their tyres. At night, I would weep

over the day's casualties, the light blue Vauxhalls,
the bright red Cortinas. But the following morning, I
was always ready, with her silent permission, to wreck more
cars, to destroy whatever it was I loved the most.

3.

One winter's evening, walking home from school,
I heard, behind me, the roar of two speeding cars, and
turned around, just in time to see them hurtle past;

a pair of brightly-coloured rally cars, side by side,
filling up the entire width of the narrow road. How I thrilled
to be so close to what might have been inevitable

death. If I had had either the inclination, or
the time, in which to act, just one step off that grassy kerb
would have ended everything. That night, in bed,

for the very first time, I was split in two; one half
of me regretting the single step I had not taken; the other
quaking at having allowed myself the thought.

For neither Love nor Money

My mother takes her purse out of her handbag,
opens it, and empties its contents into her lap. She pushes
the coins around with her index finger, picks them up,
one by one, and weighs them, individually, in her palm.
Then, she hands them to me, insisting that I keep them,
that I take them home with me when I leave. I try

to explain to her that I can't, but in my attempts
to placate her, I do take them from her and, for a moment,
hold them, tightly, in my fist. Almost immediately, she
demands that I give them back. She accuses me of stealing
them, of having come to see her only for the money. Once
they are safely back, inside her purse, the ritual begins

again; the emptying and the weighing; the offering
and the accusing; the pleading and the denials. It ends,
only when I decide to leave. Then the tears begin;
the shaking and the screaming; the swearing and the lies.
As I close the door behind me, I can hear the coins begin
to drop once more; I can hear the loose change of her sighs.

Straight from the Horse's Mouth

My mother liked to think
she knew the way horses lived;

with shiny metal jammed in their mouths;
with heavy iron nailed through their hooves;
with polished leather laid on their backs;
and always with short reins, hauling them

this way and that. She also knew how
to talk to them; breathing her breath into
their flared nostrils, and receiving theirs
in hers, in return. As a child, I both envied

and pitied those horses; having to live
so close to her; having to share in her
ridiculous whims. In the end, it was not
the lives of horses she grew to know

but the deaths of salmon; her own insides
gaffed by some invisible hook and then pulled
down and through. I would sit at the bottom
of the stairs and listen to her screaming

as the district nurse murmured to her
words of reassurance; still unsure myself
what it was, on hearing her suffering, I was
feeling; wondering if I had become

the heavy iron, or the hoof
it had been hammered through.

On finding Revenge

I went looking for revenge.
To my mother's house, I went looking
for revenge, but what I found

was a woman, who had lost her wits.
I had gone hoping to force a resolution. I had gone
hoping to clear the air, but what I found

was a vacuum. I started talking.
I sat down next to her, and I started talking. It was
hard at first, but then, the words began

to come, one by one, like water dripping
from a leaky cistern. And then, they began to run
more freely and, soon, I was caught up

in their torrent. I don't know when I began
to realise that what I was saying had no meaning;
that I was talking to the dead. All I know

was that I realised it too late. I left, having
exacted my revenge not on my mother, but myself.
I was the only one who was there; all she had

ever been had been an absence. I had grown
from victim into judge and into jury. In the end, it seemed
only natural that I should leave as the accused.

Four Crows

My mother carried her death
like another mother might carry a child.
She would not let the doctors

near her, fearing that they might
take it from her, that she might somehow
lose it prematurely. And so,

it grew in her. And though she
rarely ate, day by day, she put on weight.
And when the doctors did

examine her, they could not be
sure whether it was tumour, fluid, or wind.
In the end, it was delivered

three days early. I saw her
stomach swell for the last time, and then,
deflate. I held the invisible after-

birth in my hands. When four crows
disappeared into the branches of a nearby
oak, I knew her time had come.

The Duckbill Platypus

I am told I have
my mother's feet,
but I am clothed
in my father's fur.

I am told I have
my mother's face,
but the shape
of my father's skull.

I am told I have
my mother's veins,
but through them
runs my father's blood.

I am told I have
my mother's heart,
but it is fuelled
by my father's love.

And when my head's
above the water,
I have to listen,
and I have to watch,

but when I dive
beneath the surface,
all that is left
to me is touch.

And down there
in the darkness,
in the silence,
in the cold,

all that matters
are my feelings,
and not what
I've been told.

Star-crossed

Why are you so
obsessed with death?
She asked, as if she was
genuinely concerned.

She had a crescent moon
on her forehead and two silver stars
on her eyelids. Her boyfriend
had two blue teardrops tattooed
on his cheeks. His eyes
were gone; hers were green.

Why am I so
obsessed with death?
I could give her
no answer.

Why was she so
obsessed with the moon
and the stars? Why was he
forever weeping?